EX-
LIBRIS

AMERICAN FOUNDATION
FOR THE BLIND INC.

c, 1

Christmas Greetings
from Alice McClelland.
1940.

Miss Hoyt

The Inner Garden

By

Tilly Aston

AUTHOR OF

Singable Songs
Old-Timers
Songs Of Light
And Others

The Inner Garden

If friends come knocking at my door,
   They shall not, like the stranger, wait
For favor sought in doubting mood
   Upon the pavement at my gate.

Nor shall they sit in prim restraint,
   Where formal callers come and go:
I'll lead them to the inner yard,
   Where all my dearest blossoms blow.

And they shall gather, if they will,
   A chosen bloom, or posy fair,
The sweetest and the brightest buds
   That flourish from my planting there.

So enter to this quiet place,
   Where none but friends may hope to stray,
Where tended is my growing soul,
   That it may blossom every day.

To meet behind the lattice gate,
   Freely to share life's humble round—
Ah, truly, Friend, such humble flowers
   For you in my back yard are found.

A Christmas Song

If life's young day is at its morn,
  Or in its golden pride;
Or rich with roseate after-glow
  That paints the eventide:
If music shrills from childhood's pipe,
  Or youth's exultant lyre;
Or only echoes linger yet
  From memory's tuneful choir:
Still would I send the old salute,
  "A Merry Christmas, Friend!"
For mirth can wear a garb that fits
  Life's dawning and its end.

For present joys and future hopes
  I bid the young rejoice;
The aged for good things known of yore
  Should lift a thankful voice:
And chiefest blessing, love that burns
  Is ours, and glowing true!
Yours falls upon my heart, and mine
  Is reaching out to you.
So, Merry Christmas, Gentle Soul!
  Sweet thoughts about you throng!
And bright among them you will find
  My simple Christmas song.

The Wind Came Over the Hill

The wind came over the hill, and said,
"O'er wayside flower and pasture wide
I loitered through the countryside
To gather a gift of incense sweet,
And lay it softly at your feet."
And round me breathed the scent of bees,
Of growing grass and budding trees.

The wind came over the hill, and said,
"I crept through gullies where waters flow,
And climbed the range, where great trees grow,
To learn their music strange and new,
And softly whisper it o'er to you."
So I could hear the streamlet splash,
And solemn song of mountain-ash.

The wind came over the hill to me,
Bringing me gifts from far away,
And the loveliness born in the bush is mine,
In the city where I must stay.

Seek Not the Shadows

Seek not the shadows when the Sun is bright!
  Shadows fall on us as the clouds sail by;
Hope not to labor through the hours of night;
  Wait for the morning, till the shadows fly.

Seek not for sorrow when the joy bird sings;
  Laughter is richer than the heavy sigh:
Ask not for dirges when a mirth song rings—
  Wait for the morning, when the shadows fly.

Give me the joy, the laughter and the light,
  Day's glory shining in the radiant sky;
Why cling to sadness and the lonesome night?
  Wait for the morning, when the shadows fly.

The Only Hope
May, 1940

Nothing but night, with flowing streams of blood,
  And flashing fires of wrath, and roar of doom,
And cries of fear, and anguished suffering,
  Make hideous this hour of Stygian gloom.

For pagan madness has its grip on men,
  And all the sweets of time are put to flight,
Their room now given to the ashen fruits
  That grow upon the boughs of ruthless might.

Poor souls are crying, "Whither shall we turn?
  Is death, the unrelenting, our last friend?
Better it were to flee this Armageddon,
  And take the chance that lies beyond life's end."

But I shall hope amid my tears and sighs,
  'Mid broken strands of old-time faith in God,
For still I know I have a shepherd kind
  To keep me scathless with his staff and rod.

My Righteous Lord is not a burnt-out star,
  But flaming bright o'er the eternal sea:
Behold, a rosy glimmer stains the clouds,
  And men are yearning for the dawn to be.

5

How could I bear this present agony,
  This black abyss of wretchedness, if I
Could think the Light Resplendent dead and cold!
My faith in God and goodness shall uphold,
  Till life's fierce tribulations pass me by.

I Tread the Streets

I tread the streets at noonday,
  When crowds go jostling by;
But thoughts of thee are with me,
  And ne'er alone am I.

The veil of evening falleth
  About night's stilly brood;
Then comes thy gentle spirit
  To light my solitude.

At night, when darkness presses,
  In days when glories shine,
When toil or rest pursuing,
  'Tis joy, for thou art mine.

The Menorah

Long, long ago in Palestine,
  When Winter cold was at its height,
And turning Sun its solstice made,
  They kept the festival of light.

There Salem nestled at the foot
  Of Zion's Hill, the holy place,
Where rose Jehovah's stately fane,
  The cynosure of Israel's race.

Each opening day of Spring reborn,
  Upon the temple's topmost height,
With festive songs of grateful praise
  Was kindled the Menorah light.

It told of life's renewing flood
  Held back by Winter's chilling touch,
Of resurrected seeds that burst
  From clogging earth and death's grim clutch.

To human hearts it was a sign
  That God his mercy did renew,
As yearly doth the journeying Sun
  Shed its blest radiance from the blue.

O Happy Souls, who make a feast
  To light, when blackest midnight preys
On enterprise and confidence
  Needed to meet the coming days!

Not all is gloom, if they can lift
  Faith's bright Menorah lamp on high,
Symbol of fuller life to be,
  Where love eternal cannot die.

A Wattle-Blossom Day

This is a wattle-blossom day,
The Sun is gold against the blue,
The cloudlets soft as wattle down;
And I am rich in joy, for you
Have set upon my love its crown!
This is a wattle-blossom day.

This is a wattle-blossom day,
For life is bursting into gold,
And full of tenderness the lights.
Love's incense, like a fragrance old,
Breathes on us from the flowery heights!
This is a wattle-blossom day.

This is a wattle-blossom day,
For distant hillsides gleam and glow
With shining blossom for the Spring:
And having you, I surely know
The coming years will rapture bring!
This is a wattle-blossom day.

Everlasting Memories

The quiet Earth has bared her breast,
And to her heart thy bosom pressed;
And never more shall I behold
What her green mantle doth enfold:
Soft hands, whose touch was very dear,
Sweet lips that smiled when I was near,
Brown eyes that were a beaming light—
Vanished, and I have but the night.

How desolate my sojourn here,
My yearning heart, my secret tear!
Yet, in the silent hours I feel
Love's mystic presence round me steal;
For through those lofty halls I stray,
Where everlasting memories stay,
And sorrow sleeps, and cold despair,
O Vanished Light, for thou art there.

Where Miners Delved

One breathless day in tawny Summer
  I sought the shade of blackwoods old,
In a sequestered mountain gully,
  And came where men had delved for gold.

The pit, its black mouth yawning open,
  Grinned from encircling grassy mound,
While odors from the damp earth floated
  Up from the wet caves underground.

I dropped a stone into the darkness;
  It smote the water far below;
And from the murk a shout of laughter
  Came up to meet the noonday glow.

"Ho, Merry Gnomes!" I bent to listen:
  "What do you in that secret place?"
"Healing the ugly wounds your fathers
  Made on fair Nature's smiling face!

"Send down the stones and drifting gravel,
  Start off the trickling streams of sand,
While we break down the flooded tunnel,
  And build again the solid land."

So down I sent a snowy pebble;
  A rattling shower of gravel white
Went dancing o'er the pit's rough margin
  Like swarms of butterflies in flight.

From weathered heaps the clods I gathered,
  And sent them spinning to the deep;
A loosened boulder rumbled after,
  And vanished from the sunlit steep.

Up through the narrow shaft there rippled
  A growing din of toil and mirth,
Where hosts of restoration fairies
  Were busy mending up the Earth.

Ah, Little Rogues, in cool depths toiling,
  You ne'er have looked on Summer's face:
Your laughter tricked me into sharing
  The age-old business of your race!

But now farewell! My steps I'm bending
  Where ancient trees their coolness spread,
There I can rest, and dream, and listen,
  To hot winds humming overhead.

The Music School

Their music school was in the rustling crown
  That topped a slender eucalyptus bole;
From those green shadows leafy floated down
  A learner's effort at the song-bird's role.

The pupil was a youthful magpie heir,
  Who strove to capture all the fluty measures,
While parent birds with repetitions fair,
  Instructed him in all the songster's pleasures.

But warble and cadenza crudely broke,
  And husky crooning came instead of trill;
The Kookaburra took it for a joke,
  And shouted laughter from a near-by hill.

Ah, Maggie-bird, we folks who long to sing,
  Must let old time and nature teach us how!
We shall be singing in the coming Spring,
  Though voices break and rhythms falter now.

The Staff

The blind man said, "I dare not go
   Without my ſtaff to guide me!
There may be ruts along the road,
   A muddy ditch beside me.

"These dangers vex me not: the ſtaff
   Pointing ahead has found them;
And when I cannot ſtep across,
   I make my way around them."

And those who face the ills of life
   Without God's love to find them,
Are like the blind who wander forth,
   And leave their ſtaff behind them.

The Bridge at Beauty Creek

Where softly babbling waters
  Uphold the lily blooms,
Or whisper as the rushes wave
  Their dove-grey downy plumes;
There lies a gum-tree fallen,
  A king now prone and meek,
A bridge across the shining pool,
  The bridge at Beauty Creek.

I love the shadows falling
  On glowing Summer days,
The leaping fish, the splashing bird,
  The drifts of pearly haze:
Pure pleasure is my portion,
  Whene'er this spot I seek;
For everything is singing near
  The bridge at Beauty Creek.

And often at the sunset
  My lady comes to me,
And gentle as the pearly mist,
  And fairer far is she:
We watch the lilies floating;
  We kiss, but dare not speak,
For love's enchantment breathes around
  The bridge at Beauty Creek.

Gifts

The big tree whispered, and rustled his leaves,
And shook out his blossoms like clouds of flame;
And forth from the green Earth and sun-burnished
     air
The tiny winged creatures in myriads came.
They had heard the voice of the great tree sing
The song of the flowers, his lay of Spring—
"Mother Earth gave me her dews distilled,
Of broken bread gathered, and old made new;
Honey she gave me, my Children dear,
And I give it now to you—to you."

The bees flew busily over the flowers,
Their little wings humming their hymn of peace;
They came with the Sunrise, and tarried till noon,
And not until night did their honey-song cease.
And I heard the music of toiling bees,
That came with the fragrance adown the breeze—
"Nectar we gather from brimming flowers,
Made of the sunshine and morning dew;
Sweets the tree gave us, O Children dear,
And we give them now to you—to you."

Wayfaring Thoughts

I care not a thought for the goal
   That lies at the end of the day,
But rather the life-weary soul
   My comrade in toil by the way.

I've given my hand to The Guide,
   And know he will hold to it faſt:
Though shadows the diſtance may hide,
   I surely shall reach home at laſt.

If someone should weep by the road,
   Or shrink from intangible fears,
'Tis mine to lift part of his load,
   And mingle my own with his tears.

Perchance I may come on a friend
   Who halts to give song to his voice,
Some hope having found a bright end,
   I pause with my friend to rejoice.

So eager to crowd up the hours,
   Unwilling to let in the light,
When all the way borders of flowers
   Are spread for the traveller's delight!

There's time for the revels and song,
  For sighs and the fellowship tear;
For joyous salute to the throng,
  And kisses for lov'd ones and dear.

The goal!—Well, I know it is there,
  Where life finds the foot of the hill;
But all that is precious and rare
  Is mine, as I travel on still.

To reach that far country of peace!
  What rapture 'twill be! But I say,
The glamorous light cannot cease
  In the things that I pass by the way.

The Song of Old Age

When I am old, I would that life may be
Like the lone atoll in the gleaming sea,
Whose quiet heart the coral reefs defend
From sweeping tides, and waves that beat and rend.

There year-long Summers breathe about the palm,
And bright lagoons mirror the heavens calm,
In those clear depths the coral gardens glow,
Type of dear memories of the long ago.

And I should know that from the outer world
Through the low passes in the rampart swirled
The singing breezes and the currents cool
To stir and purify my shining pool.

Though tranquil hours the portion of my soul,
I still should hear the outer breakers roll,
Bringing some other heart to rest awhile
In the safe shelter of my sunny isle.

Here in the starry nights and quiet days,
My inward voice may chant its hymns of praise;
The voice divine may flood my waiting ear,
With God's eternal spirit very near.

Thus I should live through days of pure repose,
Which soften life's hard journey to its close;
Till, from this body obsolete, I burst
Beyond this span with limitations curst,
To toils and victories nobler than the first.

The Clock

Here, there, here, there!
  The rocking wheels within your case
Their constant oscillations show
  Upon your broad and sober face;
This, that, this, that!
  Ah, what a tale of life you beat,
Since fortune in her varied guise
  Lays gifts as diverse at our feet.

Good, bad, good, bad!
  'Tis hard to judge the things we hold,
Whether they be as worthless dross,
  Or precious as the gleaming gold:
Now, then, now, then!
  The mystic present waits the hour
When truth perfected shall be seen
  In future time's revealing flower.

You, me, you, me!
  In turn we shift the gliding hands
That point the longing, striving soul
  Through fears and fights to other lands:
Life, death, life, death!
  Thus on our spirit falls a beam,
Transmuting clay to living fire,
  And glory blest, we wait—and dream.

Quietude

There spread the verdant pasture,
  With luscious grasses tall,
The blue, bright day of Summer
  With light enfolding all:
The feeding sheep lay sprinkled
  Like lilies o'er the view,
Or clustered where the gum-trees
  Their softest shadows threw.

Near by the tiny river
  Its song of coolness breathed,
Through lacy ferns and bushes
  In sarsaparilla wreathed:
The soaring fantails warble
  Their airy music sweet,
And busy Willie Wagtails
  Their gracious song repeat.

The gum-trees wave and whisper,
  The grasses bend and sigh,
As moist airs, slowly drifting,
  Kiss them, and pass them by.
The breath of God is in it,
  This noon so calm, so fair.
This quietude is holy,
  And peace is everywhere.

Humming Tops

When I was a child I often spun
A painted top in the glowing Sun;
Its tuneful hum was a joyous sound,
As on its pivot it whirled around,
Its gay bands gleaming. But soon, too soon
The top ran down, and its pleasant tune
Was ſtilled, and the spinner toppled o'er,
A thing inert on the duſty floor.

Since then full many a top I've wound,
And set them whirling upon the ground;
I've heard their song, and their banded light
Has made some brief moment passing bright:
But all ran down when my hand was ſtayed,
Just like the hummers with which I played;
A thousand efforts, a thousand skills
Left silent, unwound, on life's far hills.

Oft I have longed a top to own,
Which, started once, would spin on alone,
Whose song and beauty would ever ſtay,
Like Earth's great orb on its age-old way.
Yet, who would forfeit the joy of winning?
'Tis God's to set the eternal spinning!
For man Endeavour is God's beheſt,
And every ſtriver will know 'tis beſt.

Madam Kangaroo

Good morning, Madam Kangaroo!
  You're early out upon the grass;
Your feet displace the shining dew,
  As through the pasture green you pass.

Where did you sleep the dark night through?
  Out in the bush-clad ranges yonder?
That is your little secret, true;
  But still, I oft about it ponder.

Does Mr. Roo your shelter share?
  Ah no, the rascal loves to roam!
But, Madam, have you not a care
  For Baby Joey left at home?

Then Madam waved her wet forepaws,
  And leapt the stone wall like a rocket.
"I have no family cares, because
  I've got my baby in my pocket."

Grandfather Gum-tree

Grandfather Gum-tree, resting, nodding, dreaming,
  I heard him whisper as the breeze went by,
Voicing dear mem'ries in his old heart teeming,
  Rain tears of Winter and Summer's glowing sky.

Grandfather Gum-tree, once so young and slender,
  Smiled at the rainbows in the river's spray;
Love-gifts he gave her, verdant leaves and tender;
  Laughing she kissed them, then sped on her way.

Grandfather Gum-tree, old and gnarled and weary,
  Stirs at the bird songs and the wind's caress;
Mem'ries of love-time still make his old heart cheery,
  E'en though age creeping has brought its lone-
    liness.

Dream, dream, and whisper,
  Your long vigil keep,
Till life is over,
  Then sigh, and fall asleep.

Tending the Flowers

The silver rain-cloud sailing low,
  Its wings above the garden spread,
A cooling shower did bestow
  Upon each thirsty flower bed:
"Come, Children, lift your drooping faces,
  That I may wash them clean and sweet!"
And from each bloom there passed the traces
  Of griming dust and wilting heat.

Then came the wind with orders brisk
  That every flower must obey,
To rock and swing, and gaily frisk,
  To bend and bow, and gently sway:
"For thus," he said, "Thy daily pleasure
  Shall be through stress to bloom and shine,
Each effort adding to the measure
  Of strength and beauty that are thine."

And last, the Sun with warm caress
  His glory shot through veiling mist,
His silent gift of light to press
  On every blossom that he kissed:
So, cloud and wind and Sun bestowing
  Each in his turn a gift of worth
Have made this beauteous, living, growing
  Flower the fairest thing on Earth.

27

Children of the Night

Tread lightly where the racing wind
  Has dropped its loot of leaves,
Where gums their worn-out bark discard,
  And moss a pattern weaves:
Go softly where this carpet brown
  In forest aisle is spread;
For here the children of the night
  Are sleeping overhead.

Through ages they have learned to fear
  The blinding glare of day;
While human children sleep and dream,
  They do their work and play:
So when you wander 'neath the trees
  To shun the noontide glow,
Think of the sleeping children there,
  And whisper as you go.

Far, far above your tiptoe height
  Is hollowed out a nest,
Where furry 'Possum curls himself
  To take his day-time rest:
And high upon a rugged limb
  The color of his coat,
Till night the drowsy mopoke stays
  His weird, elusive note.

In yonder ancient hollow log
  The bats have found a lair,
Whence, aeroplaning at the dusk,
  They hunt the wing-ed air:
The wild cat in his secret place,
  The field mice underground!—
Hush, hush, these children of the night
  Must sleep the daylight round.

The thrush is chanting to the sky
  His song of joy and grace;
The butterflies weave threads of light
  In every open space:
Should mopoke cry, or bat sail forth,
  Their joy would die of fright!
So, lightly tread, lest they should wake,
  These children of the night.

Loop Back the Curtain

Loop back the curtain of this happy day,
That Sunset glories still their crimson stay;
No night of starry peace, no burnt-out fires,
No moments yearning after dead desires.

The day has been so filled with joy and light,
Each goodly hour my loyal, obedient knight,
Bringing me spoils of pleasure gaily won,
Or golden records of some battle done.

I would not have the night, the quiet dark,
Lest in the downy gloom that living spark
Of thee, beloved one, depart alone,
On stealthy feet into the vast unknown.

While I, bereft of our communion dear,
Must follow, dragging chains of hideous fear,
That all love's glamor now must have an end,
Since I must let thee go, my best, my friend.

How lovely are the shining hours that fly
As day spreads out its dome of azure sky,
And hand in hand we share the riches wrought
By striving spirit or the pen of thought.

So leave unveiled the windows of the west,
That every ray may work its full behest,
That our unfathomed rapture still endure,
Life's present radiance and its onward lure.

The Eternal Presence

I still shall find Thee there,
   Whether I search the polar snows
Where south winds have their birth,
   And where the bright aurora glows
Above the ghostly Earth;
   Or should I seek the tropic clime,
With palms and corals rare,
   In Summer's glow or Winter's rime,
I still shall find Thee there.

I still shall find Thee there,
   Whether, O Lord, the gloom of night
Has brought the quiet hours,
   Or day outspreads its radiant light
To woo and paint the flowers;
   Whether I rest in slumber sweet,
Or wake to life's hard care,
   In tranquil night or day's fierce heat
I still shall find Thee there.

I still shall find Thee there,
   When gates of death are open thrown,
And filled my soul with dread,
   How could I venture forth alone
That shadowed way to tread!
   Yea, blessed Saviour, gentle Friend,
E'en death's dark road I dare,
   From life's first step until the end,
I still shall find Thee there.

The Inner Garden has been designed and printed by John Gartner at The Hawthorn Press, Melbourne in an edition of 600 copies during August 1940.

Lightning Source UK Ltd.
Milton Keynes UK
UKHW022048140223
417031UK00016B/149